MARY'S IDEA

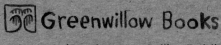

chris Raschka

Greenwillow Books
An Imprint of HarperCollins Publishers

Mary's Idea

Copyright © 2023 by Chris Raschka

All rights reserved. Manufactured in Italy. For information address HarperCollins Children's Books,
a division of HarperCollins Publishers, 195 Broadway, New York, NY 10007.
www.harpercollinschildrens.com

Ink, oil pastel, and watercolors were used on butter board to prepare the full-color art.

Library of Congress Cataloging-in-Publication Data is available.
ISBN 9780063210509 (hardcover)
23 24 25 26 27 RTLO 10 9 8 7 6 5 4 3 2 1
First Edition

Greenwillow Books

FOR RICHARD

IT WAS MARY'S

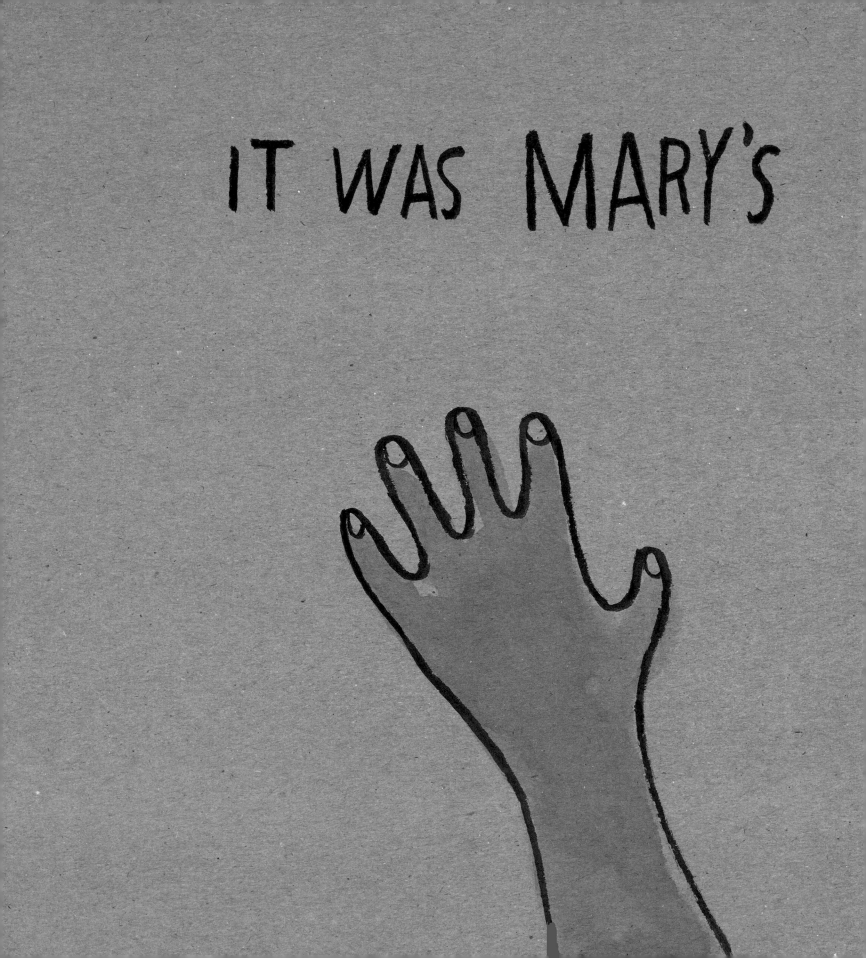

AT THREE.

TO PLAY THE PIANO

FOR ME.

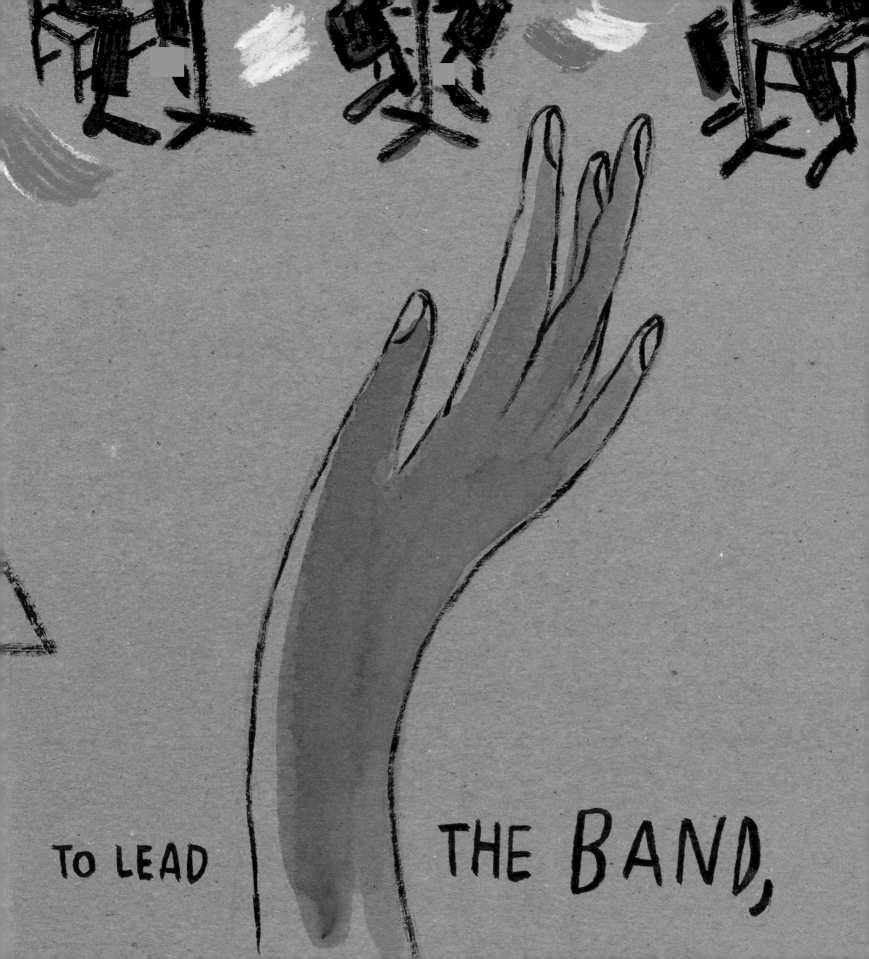

TO   SHAPE

AND MARY'S IDEAS

ARE GRAND.

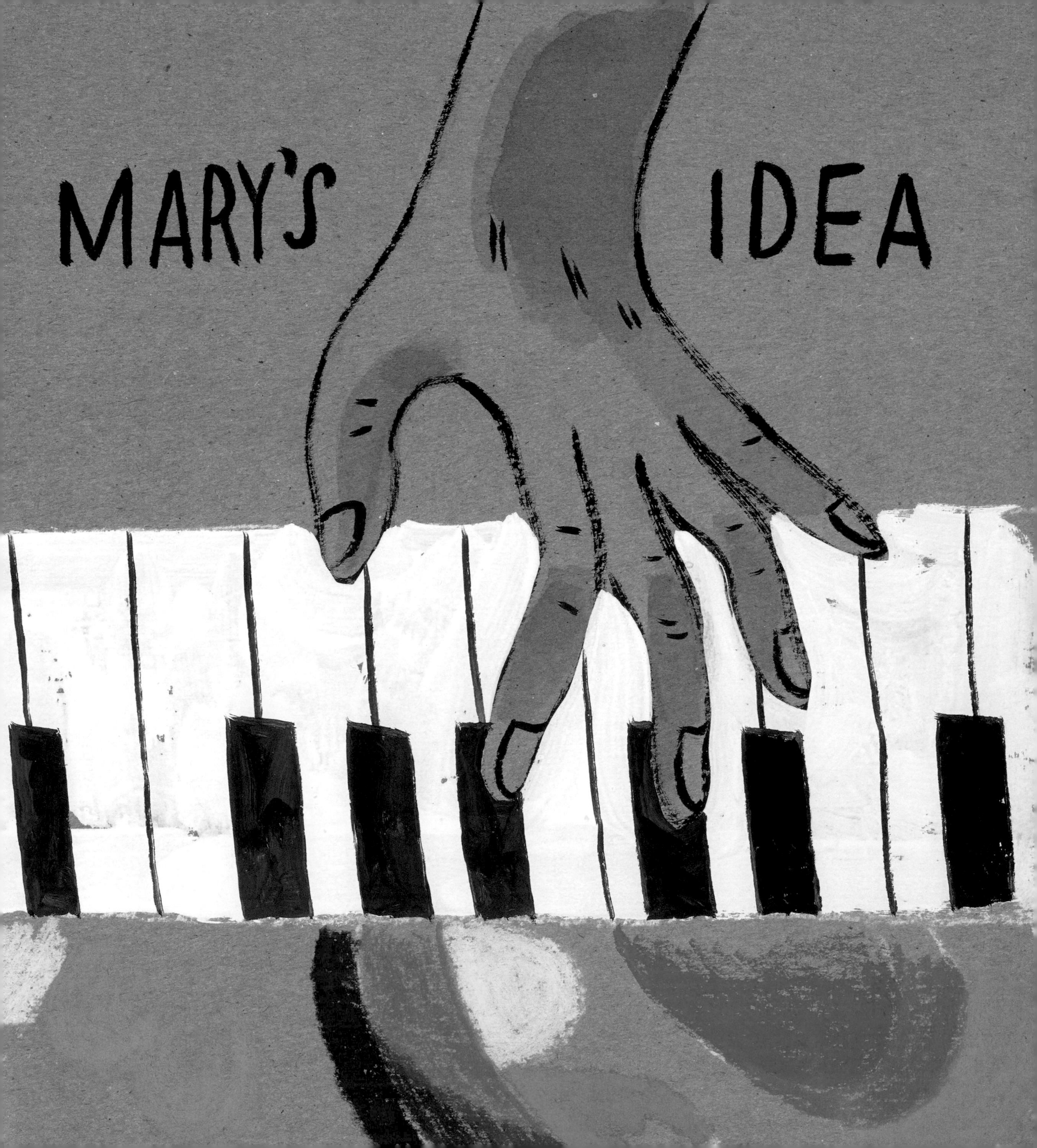
MARY'S IDEA

PLAYING

THE PIANO.

IT WAS MARY'S IDEA

TO REST.

TO START AGAIN,

FOR PEOPLE, FOR GOD,

AND ME.

MARY LOU WILLIAMS was born in Atlanta, Georgia, on May 8, 1910. Her birth name was Mary Elfrieda Scruggs. Her mother, a classical pianist, first taught her to play the piano, and then Mary taught herself. As a young girl, Mary Lou was known in Pittsburgh, Pennsylvania—where her family moved as part of the Great Migration—as the "Little Piano Girl," playing at dances, parties, and church events. Her professional career began when she was twelve. A year later she played with Duke Ellington. At nineteen, she led a band. In her twenties, she composed and arranged music for the biggest swing bands. In her thirties and forties, she headlined concerts all over the world.

Then she stopped. Saddened by the deaths of young friends such as Charlie Parker, she helped others, became a Catholic, and prayed.

At forty-seven, she began her career again. She played at festivals; she was invited to the White House; and her great mass, known today as *Mary Lou's Mass*, was performed at St. Patrick's Cathedral in New York City.

Mary Lou Williams recorded many records and composed and arranged hundreds of songs. She is an American music legend.

"YOUR ATTENTIVE PARTICIPATION, THRU LISTENING WITH YOUR EARS AND YOUR HEART, WILL ALLOW YOU TO ENJOY FULLY THIS EXCHANGE OF IDEAS, TO SENSE THESE VARIOUS MOODS, AND TO REAP THE FULL THERAPEUTIC REWARDS THAT GOOD MUSIC ALWAYS BRINGS TO A TIRED, DISTURBED SOUL AND ALL 'WHO DIG THE SOUNDS.' "
— MARY LOU WILLIAMS
Jazz for the Soul

MARY LOU WILLIAMS
1910 – 1981

For more information about Mary Lou Williams, visit www.marylouwilliams.foundation.